Reading and Writing
Learning Fun Workbook

Copyright © 2020 by Highlights for Children. All rights reserved.
Reproduction of these pages is permitted for classroom use only. Otherwise, no part of this book may be copied or reproduced without written permission of the publisher.

For information about permission to reproduce selections from this book for an entire school or school district, please contact permissions@highlights.com.

Published by Highlights Learning • 815 Church Street • Honesdale, Pennsylvania 18431
ISBN: 978-1-68437-928-6
Mfg. 10/2019
Printed in Guangzhou, Guangdong, China
First edition
10 9 8 7 6 5 4 3 2 1

For assistance in the preparation of this book, the editors would like to thank:
Vanessa Maldonado, MSEd; MS Literacy Ed. K–12; Reading/LA Consultant Cert.; K–5 Literacy Instructional Coach
Jump Start Press, Inc.

A Superior Walk

I have walked around the biggest lake in the world. That lake is Lake Superior. It is one of the five Great Lakes in the United States and Canada.

I walked about 10 miles each day. It took almost six months to go about 1,500 miles! That's like walking more than halfway across the United States!

On my hike, I passed waterfalls. I saw very old rock paintings. I even saw a moose. I also met many people. They gave me food. They invited me into their homes.

I'm not sure why I did this walk. But it is the best thing I have ever done.

> In a *personal narrative*, a writer tells a story about something that happened in his or her own life.

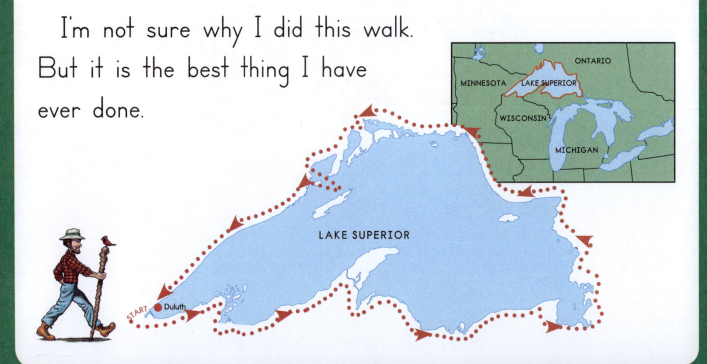

Read the personal narrative. Then answer the questions.

1. Where is Lake Superior?
   ○ in just the United States   ○ in just Canada
   ○ in both the United States and Canada

2. How many miles did the author walk? How long did it take the author to walk that far?

   _____

3. Number these sights in the order they are mentioned in the story.

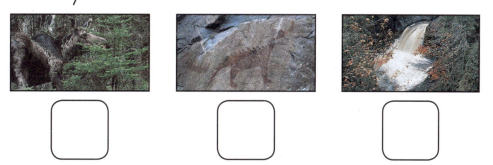

   ☐   ☐   ☐

4. Why did the author walk around Lake Superior?

   _____

Circle the 2 backpacks that match exactly.

My Best Day

Get ready to write a personal narrative about the best day of your life. Complete the story map to record your ideas.

When you write a **personal narrative**, use the pronoun **I** to tell your story.

When and where did it happen?
_____
_____

Who was with you?
_____
_____

First
_____
_____
_____

Next
_____
_____
_____

Then
_____
_____
_____

Last
_____
_____
_____

How did it make you feel?
_____
_____

Writing: Narrative: Personal Narrative

Use your story map to write your personal narrative.

Title: _____

Written by: _____

_____

_____

_____

_____

_____

_____

_____

_____

_____

_____

_____

Where can you find a lake without water? *On a map!*

Time for a Haircut

An alpaca is like a small, fluffy llama. It is raised for its woolly coat, called **fleece**. Fleece is used to make clothes and blankets. First, the fleece keeps the alpaca warm in winter. In spring, its fleece is cut. This haircut is called shearing. A haircut does not hurt you. And **shearing** does not hurt the alpaca.

Look for text features, such as captions and bold print, to find information easily.

An electric razor is used for shearing.

The fleece is combed with a wooden paddle. This paddle is called a **card**. Its short, steel teeth remove dirt, hay, and grass.

A **spinning wheel** turns fleece into yarn.

Alpaca yarn is soft and warm. It was used to make this hat.

Read the informational text. Answer the questions.

1. What is alpaca wool called?
   _____
   _____

2. What does **shearing** mean?
   _____
   _____

3. How does a **card** help when making alpaca yarn?
   _____
   _____

4. What does a **spinning wheel** do?
   _____
   _____

5. Name two things that can be made from alpaca fleece.
   _____
   _____

Which winter hat does NOT have a match?

Picture Perfect!

Draw pictures about getting a haircut. Under each picture, add a **caption**. Write important words or words that need definitions in a darker color, or **bold**.

Using pictures, captions, and other text features can help make information clearer.

Informational Text: Photo Essay

Write the main text for your "photo" essay. Then add captions and any definitions for the information you show in your pictures.

Title: _____

Written by: _____

_____
_____
_____
_____
_____
_____
_____
_____
_____
_____
_____

Circle the differences you see between these pictures.

Racing the Beast

Made-up stories that could happen in real life are called realistic fiction.

The beast **growls** at the bottom of the hill. I **peer** into the morning mist. I can't see anything. But I know it's coming.

I grab my little brother's hand. He's only five. "Hurry!" I yell.

We run. My brother **skids** in a puddle. His boot cracks the thin ice. He stops to **poke** it with a toe.

I **nudge** him. "Run!"

Now the beast **bursts** out of the mist. Its eyes **glare**. It **lunges** up the road. We'll never make it!

The beast sees us! It **screeches**. Then it stops to purr and wait.

We keep running. My brother stumbles, but I help him up.

The beast is almost as long as our house. Its mouth opens wide. My brother steps into it bravely. Then I climb inside. Then the beast slams its mouth shut.

I look up. I'm still **gasping** for breath.

"You're pushing your luck, Matt!" says a woman in the driver's seat. "Next time, I'm not waiting. It will be a long walk to school!"

She grips the steering wheel and gets the beast going. With a roar, our school bus rattles and rumbles to our school.

Reading Comprehension: Literature: Realistic Fiction

Read the realistic story. Then answer the questions.

1. Who is telling the story?
   _____

2. How do you think the brothers feel at the beginning of the story?
   _____

3. What will happen if the brothers can't beat the beast?
   _____
   _____

4. What is the beast? What did you think the beast was at the beginning of the story?
   _____
   _____

5. Were you surprised by the ending? Why?
   _____
   _____
   _____
   _____

What do you call a hairy beast that is lost?

A where-wolf!

Follow the Clues!

Do you know the meaning of these words from the story on page 10? Read the story again for clues! Then draw a line from each word to its definition.

Context clues are words in the text that can help you figure out the meaning of a difficult word.

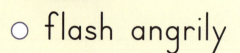

growls ○	○ flash angrily
peer ○	○ explodes
skids ○	○ rushes
poke ○	○ taking quick breaths
nudge ○	○ slides
bursts ○	○ screams
glare ○	○ push gently
lunges ○	○ look closely
screeches ○	○ angry rumbles
gasping ○	○ jab

Vocabulary: Context Clues

Read the story below. Write words from the word box that mean the same as the words in bold. Use clues in the sentences.

> arrived   attention   calm   effort   haste   present

I didn't pay **careful notice** (_____) to the clock. I **came to a place after traveling** (_____) at the corner just in time to catch our bus. My teacher asked me to **give in public** (_____) my book report to the class. I felt **not scared** (_____) about reading it out loud. Writing the report wasn't easy, but it was worth the **hard work** (_____) Oops! In my **speed or hurry** (_____) to catch the bus, I forgot the report at home!

What silly things do you see?

Problem Solved!

Get ready to write a realistic story. Complete the story map to record your ideas.

A good story has a problem and characters who try to solve the problem.

Characters
_____
_____
_____

Setting
_____
_____

Problem: What is wrong?
_____

How do the characters try to solve the problem?
_____
_____
_____

How does the story end?
_____
_____

My Story

Use your story map to write your realistic story.

Title: _____

Written by: _____

Help Finn get to his school of fish!

Shooting Stars

Informational text gives facts that can be proved.

"Shooting stars" aren't stars at all. They are really "shooting rocks"! These rocks are called **meteors**.

A meteor's story starts more than 4 billion years ago. That's when the sun and planets formed in a cloud of **gas** and dust. Bits of dust near the sun stuck together. They formed rocks.

Many rocks clumped together. Some formed planets close to the sun. Other rocks did not become part of planets. These rocks are called **asteroids**. Asteroids can be as big as trucks. Very big ones are hundreds of miles wide.

Asteroids are part of the **solar system**. Some **orbit** the sun and pass close to Earth. Asteroids can crash into each other. Pieces of rock break off. Many pieces are no bigger than a grain of sand. Sometimes, the rocks enter Earth's **atmosphere**. They move very fast and heat up. Some rocks land on Earth. But many rocks burn up. Then we see a flash of light in the sky. That's a shooting star!

Don't know the meaning of some of these words? Turn to the glossary on page 18.

Read the report. Answer the questions.

1. "Shooting stars" are not really stars. What are they?
   _____
   _____

2. What is an asteroid?
   _____
   _____

3. How big can an asteroid be?
   _____
   _____

4. How does an asteroid become a meteor?
   _____
   _____

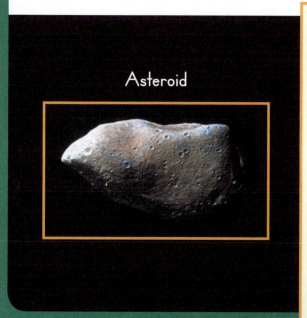

Asteroid

Meteor Spotting

You don't need a telescope to see shooting stars—just your eyes. The best times are clear, dark nights in August, in a wide-open area away from bright lights. Lie on a chair or blanket. Then scan the sky. You might want to keep a chart of how many shooting stars you see on what dates. Then try again next year on the same dates and compare numbers.

Space to Learn

Like a **dictionary**, a glossary is a list of definitions. But it defines words related to one subject. Use this glossary for the report on page 16.

GLOSSARY

asteroid: A rocky, planet-like body that circles the sun

atmosphere: The gases around Earth or other planets

gas: A form of matter that is not solid or liquid

meteor: A rock that enters our atmosphere and burns up

orbit: To move around another object

solar system: A sun and the planets, moons, and other bodies that travel around it

Some words are related to science, social studies, or other school subjects. You may need a dictionary to find the meanings of these words.

Circle the crescent moon and 7 other objects in this Hidden Pictures puzzle.

 crescent moon
 slice of pizza
 scissors
 football
 baby's bottle
 book
 ice-cream cone
 fried egg

Vocabulary: Content Area Words

Lost in Space

Some words are missing from these outer-space sentences. Use the glossary on page 18 to fill in each word.

1. It takes one year for the Earth to completely _____ the sun.

2. Earth's _____ is made up of nitrogen, oxygen, and other gases.

3. Jupiter is the largest planet in our _____ _____.

4. A rock that did not become part of a planet but still circles the sun is called an _____.

Can you spot the asteroid? Then help astronaut Amal find her way back to the space station.

Blast Off!

Get ready to write a report about a favorite planet or another object in space. Write your ideas in the organizer below.

Introduction
_____
_____
_____
_____

Body: facts and definitions
_____
_____
_____
_____
_____

Conclusion
_____
_____
_____
_____

A *report* gives facts about a topic.

Say this tongue twister five times fast: *Stacy steers by the stars in space.*

Use your organizer to write your report.

Title: _____

Written by: _____

_____

_____

_____

_____

_____

_____

_____

_____

_____

Circle the differences you see between these pictures.

An Indian Folktale

Every day, Heron went fishing in the river. Hummingbird fished, too. But fish were becoming hard to find.

"There are not enough fish for both of us," said Heron. "One of us should find something else to eat."

"Let's settle this with a race," said Hummingbird. Hummingbird could fly very fast.

"OK," said Heron. "Let's race to that tree. The winner will eat fish. The loser must eat something else."

The race began. Heron flapped his big, heavy wings. Flap! Flappety! Flop!

Hummingbird flew quickly. Zip! Zing! Zoom!

Soon Hummingbird got tired. "I will take a nap," he thought. "I have lots of time. Heron is far behind."

But when Hummingbird woke up, Heron was way ahead! Hummingbird zoomed to the old tree. But he was too late! Heron got there first.

That is why Heron eats fish and Hummingbird sips from flowers.

A folktale is a story that has been passed down by storytellers.

An Aesop's Fable

One day, Hare made fun of Tortoise for being slow.

"Do you ever get anywhere?" he asked.

"Yes, and I get there sooner than you think," said Tortoise. "Let's race. I'll prove it."

Hare laughed. But he said yes, just for the fun of it. They asked Fox to be the judge. Fox drew a starting line and a finish line. "On your mark, get set, go!" he shouted.

Soon, Hare was out of sight. How could he make Tortoise feel silly for racing him? "I'll lie down for a nap," he thought. "I'll zoom away when Tortoise catches up."

Meanwhile, Tortoise kept going, slowly but steadily. After a while, he passed Hare. But Hare slept on.

When Hare woke up at last, Tortoise was near the finish line! Hare ran as fast as he could. But he was too late. Tortoise crossed the finish line. He had won the race!

Can you find the 8 objects in this Hidden Pictures puzzle? Take your time!

ring

flowerpot

microphone

swim goggles

sandwich

harmonica

yo-yo

light bulb

Two Tales

Compare to tell how things are alike. Contrast to tell how they are different.

1. Who are the characters in each story?
   _____
   _____

2. Why did the fastest character in each story lose the race?
   _____
   _____

3. How is the race different in each story?
   _____
   _____

4. What does this picture tell you about Hummingbird?
   _____
   _____

5. What is the lesson of both stories?
   _____
   _____

6. Do you think the ending of one story is stronger than the other? Why or why not?
   _____
   _____
   _____
   _____

Write your own folk tale, using the same lesson as the two folk tales you read. Set the story as if it were happening today.

Title: _____

Written by: _____

_____
_____
_____
_____
_____
_____
_____
_____
_____
_____
_____
_____
_____
_____
_____
_____
_____

> Knock, knock. *Who's there?* Ketchup. *Ketchup who?* Ketchup with me and I'll tell you!

Writing: Narrative: Folk Tale

Snooze News

*A **process text** describes how something happens in order.*

At night, you climb into bed and close your eyes. Then before you know it, it's morning! What happens in between? As you sleep, parts of your body rest.

Meanwhile, muscles and other parts build and repair cells. Your brain is also busy. It sorts out and stores information. So counting sheep to fall asleep is probably not a good idea. It keeps your brain too busy!

Each night, you go through different levels of sleep. These cycles are called stages. You sleep lightly in the first two stages. A noise might wake you. Stage 3 comes next. You sleep more deeply. You are less aware of sounds and your senses. Your heartbeat and breathing slow down, too.

Finally, you enter the last stage. This stage is called REM sleep. REM stands for "rapid eye movement." Your eyes move back and forth under your eyelids! Your heartbeat and breathing speed up. Your brain is busy. This is when you dream the most.

Every 90 minutes or so, you repeat stages 2, 3, and REM in order. In 9 hours of sleep, you go through this cycle 6 times!

Read the process text about sleep. Then answer the questions.

1. What does your body do while you sleep?
   _____
   _____

2. What happens first after you fall asleep?
   _____
   _____

3. What happens next?
   _____
   _____

4. When are you most likely to dream?
   _____

5. How many times will you go through the different stages of sleep in one night?
   _____

Circle the differences you see between these pictures.

Dream It Up

A process paragraph is a how-to in paragraph form.

Dream up a process paragraph. Write your ideas here. You might tell about what you do to get ready for bed.

Topic
_____
_____

First
_____
_____

Next
_____
_____

Then
_____
_____

Last
_____
_____

Writing: Informational Text: Process Paragraph

Write a process paragraph using your dreamy ideas from page 28.

Title: _____

Written by: _____

_____
_____
_____
_____
_____
_____
_____
_____

Did you know koalas can sleep up to 22 hours a day? Help each koala find its bed.

Wish You Were Here!

Sofia sent Noah this letter with scrambled words. Use words from the word box to replace the highlighted, scrambled words and figure out Sofia's real message.

A **friendly letter** is written to someone the writer knows.

calm	coat	dawn	Dear	friend
Life	live	note	ocean	pier	pool
rose	shore	soak	surf	tide	time

March 24

(Ared) _____ Noah,

   I'm writing you this (teon) _____ from the sandy (rhose) _____! (Feil) _____ is good at the beach. I think you would like to (ilev) _____ here. It's so warm all the (temi) _____ that you never need a (acto) _____.

   Yesterday, the (nacoe) _____ was too (malc) _____ to (rufs) _____, so we decided to (koas) _____ in the (lopo) _____. Today, we (eors) _____ at (nawd) _____ to watch the sunrise from the (prei) _____ as the (idet) _____ rolled in.

       Your (nifred) _____,
       Sofia

Hello from the rhose!

Read Sofia's letter to Noah. Then answer the questions.

1. What is the date on the **heading** of the letter?
   _____

2. What **salutation** or **greeting** does Sofia use?
   _____

3. How does Sofia feel about the beach?
   _____

4. Why does Sofia think Noah would want to live there?
   _____

5. What are some things that Sofia did on vacation?
   _____
   _____

6. How does Sofia close her letter?
   _____

7. Circle the **signature** of the letter.

What is the best kind of letter to get on a hot day?
Fan mail!

A Letter to a Friend

Think about a favorite place you have visited. Write why you enjoyed it and why a friend might like it, too.

An **opinion** is what a person thinks about something. A **reason** tells why the person thinks a certain way.

Reason 1
_____
_____
_____
_____
_____
_____

My favorite place is
_____
_____

Reason 2
_____
_____
_____
_____
_____
_____

Reason 3
_____
_____
_____

Writing: Opinion: Friendly Letter

Write your friendly letter using your wheel of words.

_____

_____

_____

_____

_____

_____

_____

_____

_____

_____

_____

_____

What silly things do you see?

Morning on the Pond

Sunlight shimmers on the smooth pond. My reflection smiles back up at me. The sweet scent of fern floats on the soft breeze. Plants sway on their skinny stems. I dip my paddle up and down, like a windmill. My yellow kayak glides. That startles a plump frog! It leaps into the cool water. Another bright green frog flicks out its long tongue. It nabs a buzzing bug. A dragonfly swoops down nearby. Then stops in midair. I see other tiny helicopters everywhere!

A **description** uses words to tell what something is like.

Can you find 20 dragonflies at this pond?

Read the description. Then answer the questions.

1. Where does the storyteller see her reflection?
   _____

2. What is paddling a kayak like?
   _____

3. What makes the frog leap into the water?
   _____

4. What words helped you "see" or "feel" things in the story?
   _____
   _____

5. Do you know now what it's like to be by a pond? Why or why not?
   _____
   _____
   _____
   _____
   _____
   _____

Follow the paths to see what each frog had for lunch.

Made in the Shade

Read each set of words. Draw an **X** over the one word that does NOT have almost the same meaning.

1. **shimmers** sparkles shouts shines
2. **sway** rock wobble hit
3. **startles** begins scares surprises
4. **plump** fat chubby juicy
5. **flicks** snaps films flips
6. **nabs** sleeps catches takes
7. **swoops** dives dips slows

Which shadow really came from this tree?

Vocabulary: Shades of Meaning

Berry Good!

Choose a more interesting word from the word box to replace each word in bold. Write it on the line.

> chilly   crouch   dribbles   gooey
> low   nibble   perfect   pluck   smeared

It's a **cool** (_____) spring morning on the strawberry farm. We **bend** (_____) down to **pick** (_____) the fruit from the **short** (_____) bushes. I choose a **good** (_____) one! As I **eat** (_____) it, the juice **drips** (_____) down my chin. My brother's face is already **spread** (_____) a **sticky** (_____) red!

Circle the 10 objects in this Hidden Pictures puzzle.

- balloon
- spoon
- mushroom
- bow tie
- whisk broom
- slice of pie
- pot of gold
- violin
- rolling pin
- ice-cream sandwich

Let It Snow!

Think of something that you do or see in the winter. Using your five senses, write words here that describe your idea.

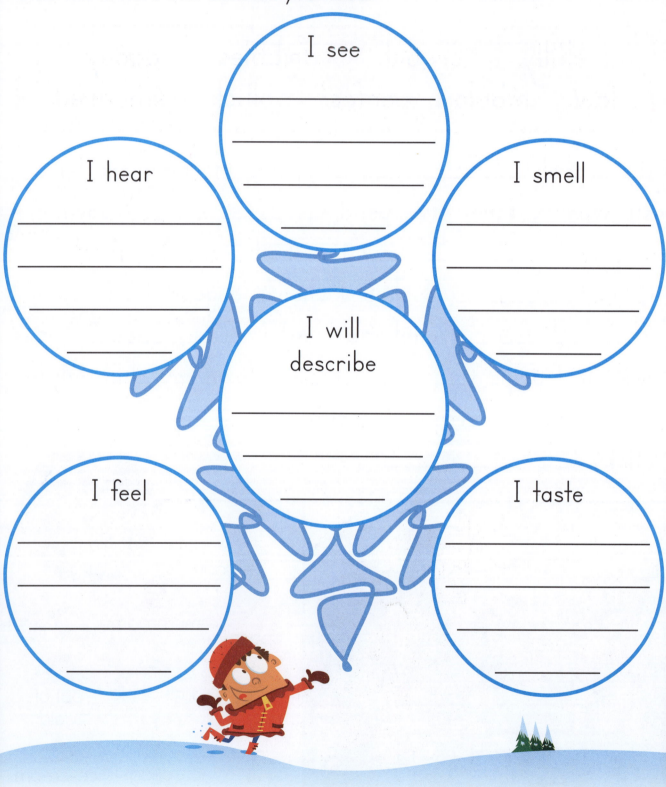

Write your description from the ideas in your sense-sational snowflake.

Title: _____

Written by: _____

_____

_____

_____

_____

_____

_____

_____

_____

_____

_____

Can you number these pictures in order?

Summer Nights

On summer nights, when soft winds sigh,
And countless stars caress the sky,
I leave my window open wide
And listen to the world outside:

The crooning crickets, lowing cows,
The creaking of the cedar boughs,
The croaking frogs, the whip-poor-wills,
Coyotes yipping in the hills.

Their voices linger on the breeze,
Familiar sounds that soothe and ease.
On summer nights, I close my eyes,
Nestled in nature's lullabies.

A poem uses colorful words to make a reader feel a certain way or to paint pictures in a reader's mind.

Say this tongue twister five times fast: *Coyote howls loudly at the moon.*

Read the poem. Then answer the questions.

1. When does the poem take place?
   _____

2. Which animals does the poet hear?
   _____
   _____

3. Write the words that sound like noises.
   _____
   _____

4. What do you think the word *lowing* means?
   ○ short   ○ mooing   ○ snorting

5. What is another word for *boughs*?
   ○ bows   ○ trunks   ○ branches

6. What does the poet think the night noises are like?
   _____

7. How does the poem make you feel?
   _____
   _____
   _____
   _____

Sounds Right!

1. Write some rhyming words from the poem on page 40 or make up your own.

   _____

   _____

   _____

2. The words *crooning* and *crickets* have the same beginning *cr* sound. Write some other words you know with the same beginning sound.

   _____

   _____

3. Circle each sound word in this poem.

   ### Piano Recital

   My heart pounds.
   Boom, boom, boom.
   I look around the room.
   It's my turn next. Gulp! Eek!
   I stand up. Crackle, creak.
   You can do this, I think.
   Just press keys:
   Plink, plink, plink.

Circle the 2 pianos that match.

Vocabulary: Sound Words

Rumble-Grumble

Circle the colorful words in this poem. Then write words that have almost the same meaning as each word. Or write a similar line using your own colorful words.

Colorful words help readers know what something is like.

A gloomy gray and rainy day,
_____

Too cold and cloudy out to play.
_____

The lightning lightens up my room,
_____

And thunder crashes, boom-ba-boom!
_____

There's a rattle-tattle on the roof.
_____

My dog lets out a wimpy woof.
_____

Outdoors, a rumble-grumble storm,
_____

But in my room, we're safe and warm.
_____

Vocabulary: Colorful Words

Poem Pages

Plan a poem that tells about an animal or a place in nature. Write your topic in the center. Make notes for colorful words and sound words in the other circles.

A poem often gives the poet's feelings and opinions about a topic.

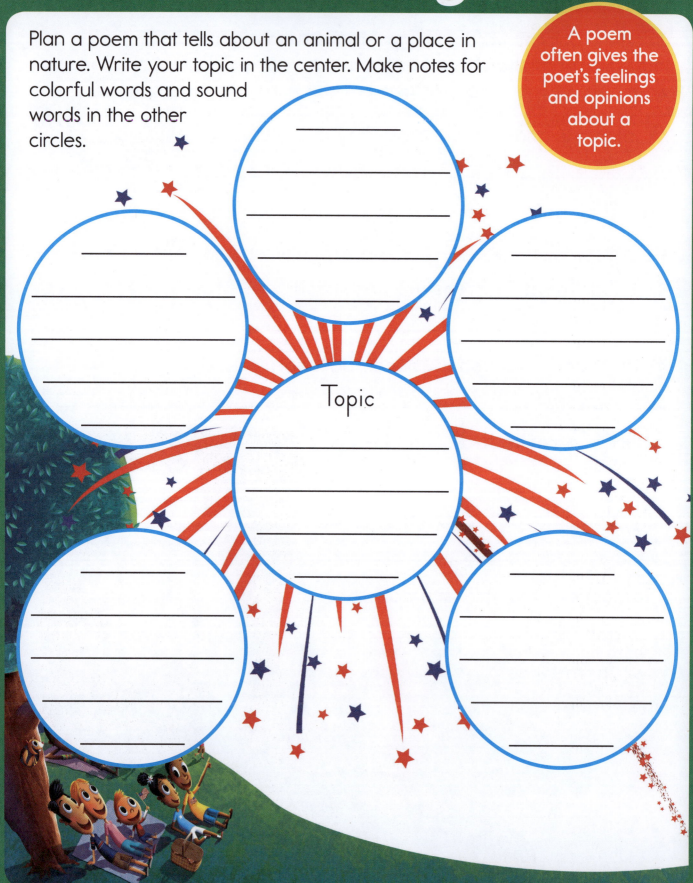

Write a poem using your colorful words and sound words.

Title: _____

Written by: _____

SECOND GRADE 2

Congratulations!

_____
(your name)

worked hard
and finished the
Reading and Writing
Learning Fun Workbook

Highlights

Answers

Inside Front Cover

Page 7
Time for a Haircut

1. Alpaca wool is called fleece.
2. Shearing means cutting the fleece off of the alpaca.
3. A card's short steel teeth are good for combing out dirt, hay, and grass.
4. A spinning wheel turns alpaca fleece into yarn.
5. You can make many things from alpaca wool, including hats, gloves, sweaters, and socks.

Pages 3-4
A Superior Walk

1. Lake Superior is in both the United States and Canada
2. The author walked 1,500 miles It took the author almost six months.
3.

4. The author is not sure why he or she walked around Lake Superior.

Page 9
Picture Perfect

Page 11
Racing the Beast

1. Matt is telling the story.
2. I think the brothers feel rushed.
3. If they can't beat the beast, they will miss the bus to school.
4. The beast is the school bus.

Pages 12-13
Follow the Clues!

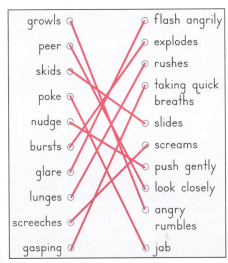

I didn't pay attention to the clock. I arrived at the corner just in time to catch our bus. My teacher asked me to present my book report to the class. I felt calm about reading it out loud. Writing the report wasn't easy, but it was worth the effort. Oops! In my haste to catch the bus, I forgot the report at home!

Page 15
Problem Solved!

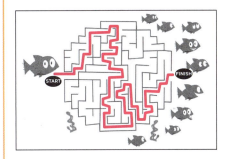

Answers

Pages 16–17
Shooting Stars

1. "Shooting stars" are rocks called meteors.
2. Asteroids are rocks that did not become part of planets.
3. Asteroids can be as big as trucks.
4. Asteroids become meteors when they crash into each other and rocks break off.

Page 18
Space to Learn

Page 19
Lost in Space

1. It takes one year for the Earth to completely orbit the sun.
2. Earth's atmosphere is made up of nitrogen, oxygen, and other gases.
3. Jupiter is the largest planet in our solar system.
4. A rock that did not become part of a planet but still circles the sun is called an asteroid.

Page 21
Blast Off!

Page 23
An Aesop's Fable

Page 24
Two Tales

1. The characters are Heron and Hummingbird and Tortoise and Hare.
2. The fastest characters in each story lost because they took naps.
3. One story has the characters flying in a race, and the other has the characters running in a race.
4. The picture tells you that Hummingbird is smaller than Heron.
5. The lesson of both stories is that the best way to win a race is to keep going.

Page 27
Snooze News

1. While you sleep, your body rests, builds and repairs cells, and sorts and stores information.
2. When you first fall asleep, you sleep lightly.
3. Next, you sleep more deeply. Your heartbeat and breathing slow down.
4. You are most likely to dream during REM sleep.
5. You can go through the different stages of sleep 6 times in 9 hours.

Page 29
Dream it Up

Page 30
Wish You Were Here!

Dear Noah,

    I'm writing you this note from the sandy shore! Life is good at the beach. I think you would like to live here. It's so warm all the time that you never need a coat.

    Yesterday, the ocean was too calm to surf, so we decided to soak in the pool. Today, we rose at dawn to watch the sunrise from the pier as the tide rolled in.

                   Your friend,
                     Sofia